One Day the Birds Will Explain Everything

Mark Bromberg

Parson's Porch Books

One Day the Birds Will Explain Everything
ISBN: Softcover 978-1-960326-98-0

Copyright © 2024 by Mark Bromberg

Parson's Porch Books is an imprint of Parson's Porch *&* Company (PP*&*C) in Cleveland, Tennessee. PP*&*C is a self-funded charity which earns money by publishing books of noted authors, representing all genres. Its face and voice is **David Russell Tullock** (dtullock@parsonsporch.com).

Parson's Porch *&* Company *turns books into bread & milk* by sharing its profits with the poor.

www.parsonsporch.com

One Day the Birds Will
Explain Everything

With thanks to all who have helped
with their lively conversation, sharp eye,
and enduring friendship,
this collection is especially for Dac

... and it's no, nay, never
no nay never no more
will I play the wild rover
no, never no more

Acknowledgements

Many thanks are due the poetry community Athens Word of Mouth, a continuing source of inspiration and opportunity. In addition, several individuals have offered invaluable support and suggestions. Bob Ambrose, Penny Noah, David Oates, and Eugene Bianchi have all been instrumental in sharpening my poems and clarifying my meaning.

The creative assistance offered at regular gatherings in the past ten years is worth celebrating. Many thanks to Firemouth Salon, Donderos' Kitchen, Covid-era Zoom calls, Hendershots, and front-porch readings 2020-2022 are all remembered with appreciation and fondness.

Thanks are also given to publications and venues where some materials have appeared / been performed: ARTini's / ATHICA / A Prairie Home Companion / Bellemeade Books / Big Bridge / Black Eye / Boom Athens / Brick / Drunken Boat / Eco-lab / Emory University (Atlanta, GA) / Georgia Review / Globe Athens / Hendershots / Jack / Literary Kicks / Mollyhouse / Off the Page (WSKG-FM, Binghamton) / Open Salon / Psychedelic Press UK (London) / Reality Studio / Word of Mouth (Athens, GA) / Word of Mouth (Cincinnati, OH) / Wordland (WUGA-FM, Athens)

Cover illustration by Fumitake Uchida

Poems

"Utopias are steadily on the decline."

(Katherine Anne Porter)

Introduction

On Poetry (For Mark Bromberg)

Though,
With me,
It is always about line length,
And
Connections
(with ELECTRONICS
No less).

Lowell said it,
At the rainbows end,
Only by getting rid of things
Can you let
THINGS
In.
(Where was Olson in this?)
"It is undone business..."

Which brings us back to the lightning bugs.

Steve Maurer
May 2023

Stone strike bone

"To build out of sound the walls of the city ..." (Charles Olson)

Flint strike spark, stone strike bone.
      Sometimes it's the thought more often than not
keeps us from finding our way home:
      Cain slew Abel, and all that begot.

Well we would if we could but we can't so we won't,
      and it's *piss off* and *kiss this and rocks in your head,*
saying *I do* when we know that we don't.
      Now we're all stuck with each other. Instead,

what kind of planet do you want to inhabit?
      Earth must feel like a childless mother
with all that we grab at.
      This is our only, there is no other.

Build high around you 'til all that you hear
      is sound above you, so pure and clear.
There's blood on the sun that can't be undone.
      Offer in hope all you hold dear.

Flint strike spark, stone strike bone,
      and a spider's thread to show the way home.

New year

The promise of utopias
proves I can carry on:

Mondays are all inside my head,
Tuesdays I pay bills instead.

Wednesday the cat
vomits on the rug.

Thursday is a promising drug;
Friday at last stumbles into view.

Saturday -- and everything new.
Sunday as it ever was:

I find myself in pause
between, beyond, because.

The poems that get away

Words run down drains and disappear in smoke,
      entire poems vanish when the cat wants out.
Rhymes get lost at the bar, and quick scribbled lines,
      on napkins soaked with good Guinness stout.

Look for the poems that wander away,
      search while you curse til the moon goes down.
That perfect verse is gone, long gone,
      to some lost word-yard on the outskirts of town.

The "delete" key is an unforgiving judge.
      Curse the computer when it takes the power hit
and steals fifty of your best lines' wit.
      Then make coffee as black as sludge,
begin a new poem as quickly as you can.
      Poems that run away won't run back again.

One day the birds will explain everything

You won't need the drink, the cigarette,
>   the news will be background noise.

You will wait at 3 a.m. for the nightingale
>   to bring day's first word, and understand

the day stretches ahead with limitless possibility,
>   its wealth of sun,

and the clouds will be golden-lined.
>   There will be no pennies from heaven,

which will seem unfortunate at first.
>   No one who listens to birds for their wisdom

will need gold or silver to line their pockets
>   when the songs of the birds are limitless.

Life sentences

Relationships in the mirror are closer than they appear.
> *You can expect to hear back in a week or a year.*

The heart you requested disappeared in the mail.
> *A replacement will be sent to you without fail.*

Be kind to animals, in-laws, and neighbors.
> *Their tricks will provide relief from your labors.*

If you would like to speak with someone, please hold.
> *With luck your youth will never grow old.*

Work toward sanity, but enjoy an occasional yelp.
> *A drink may save you from professional help.*

Don't hurry the future, it comes without pause.
> *We regret any inconvenience this may cause.*

Joy Joy Beauty & Party Supply

Across an eyesore of asphalt
on Hawthorne Avenue in Athens GA
a storefront offers "Joy Joy Beauty
& Party Supply" in big, bold letters.
A fella could have a pretty good time
with all that, I think, even though
the windows display an ancient collection
of wigs and hair extensions, along with
photos featuring glittering nail appliqués.

Faces smile from sun-bleached posters,
the models with hairstyles fashionable
ten years ago or more. I could
likely do without such refinements
to my promised party mood,
but I admire the store's instance
that joy is available there
with the doubling of abundance
that Chinese language allows.

I pass the shop at least once a day
and smile: *joy joy beauty*
has become my daily affirmation.
I wonder if any supply of party horns
and hats, gift wrap and wigs,
could ever surround life
with so much amplified happiness,
or if my own beat and battered heart
would survive such a gift
without breaking completely in two.

Sometimes the most
courageous thing to do
is to walk down the street.

Sometimes the most
outrageous thing people do
is let go the desire for control.

This might get you killed
but it may get you kissed.

Such tough philosophical questions
are answered by the promise
of *joy joy beauty* every day
even when I have a difficult time
admitting the possibility.

I keep a close watch on my heart,
but often I need some multiplied joy.
I know where to find the source
on Hawthorne Avenue in Athens GA:
I catch the Number 5 bus
past the Salvation Army Family Store,
next to the Car Quest Auto Supply,
in a broken-down building shared
with the Golden Comb barber shop
and the Zebra Room. *Joy joy beauty*
is waiting patiently for me,
across the corner from Walgreen's

What to require of love

"Imagination is the power of the mind over the possibilities of things." (Wallace Stevens)

That it speak individually and universally.
    That it cross imaginary borders.
That it transcend thought and action.
    That it is greater than an electrical force.

It should be more than emotion.
    It should be more than physical act.
It should be alive in head as well as loins.
    It should bind humans together.

That it give life to others.
    That it is beyond human expression.
That it express more than life itself.
    That it express the world complete.

That it be serious and playful.
    That it is foolish and heart-felt.
That it be forever and immediate.
    That it is both elemental and ephemeral.

It should be earth and air, fire and water.
    It should come to us unbidden.
It should be all of these, all of these,
    and nothing at all.

Unexpected

The radio is teaching my cat
how to invest in the stock market

The power company is threatening
to turn off my thoughts

The postman keeps putting
ideas in the mailbox that aren't mine

What kind of days are these
that have no name but today

Politicians are saying I should go
and do something to someone

That it's right to cast the first stone
if I have more stones in my pocket

It seems more useful to recite poetry
or shout bus schedules at strangers

but I'm too busy these days
learning to speak butterfly

I do not ask for much

Some people think
that poetry should be
adorned or complicated.

I'll take the simple statement
in plain speech
with some thought behind it.

If there is a message
I want to catch it
without a baseball mitt.

That is not to say
I don't enjoy watching
a home run ball sail over my head

but I want that poem
to be so spectacular a home run
that I spend the day happily

thinking about it.

Very well

"Very well, I contradict myself" (Walt Whitman)

How boring it must be
to be the same person all the time.

It's human to hold contradictions,
to be of two minds.

"I'm this, I'm that,"
the philosopher Moondog sang

as he stood on a Manhattan corner
in the 1950s,

confronting passers-by
with essential duality,

the happy and the sad,
the last and the next,

the forever and the never:
the Coldspot refrigerator in the kitchen

and the bomb at Los Alamos.

Contradictions are the loom of life,
the weave that binds us

in the light of day
and love at night

Almost

I'm the man I see in the mirror each morning.
If anyone were to look at me as I see myself
there would be the merest smile
as I studied in the University library
at Syracuse in the winter of 1973,
ready to do something else, be anywhere
but there. Almost done.

I'm somewhere else now
and almost fifty years later, happy still,
but with smile more wan
(poetics would make me add "and pale,"
but in that reverse order to indicate
I know what I'm doing, poetry-wise).

It's the wisdom of the ages settling like dust,
my own wisdom at least – see what I did there?
The dust of wisdom as a metaphor
for my own gray hair? -- having done all I could
to be the inner rock star, with gin in the glass
and a gimlet eye to survey the wreckage

with a knowing sigh, as if to say
well, that was a pretty good start
as I close in on the age of 70.
I still laugh in surprise at the face that looks
back from the mirror. Almost done.

Covid party days

When people phone me these days
        they ask "what are you doing?"
as if I have a wild party in mid-swing,

Mick Jagger spilled his martini on the rug,
        Scarlett Johansson is romping on the couch
with Brad Pitt.

I smile at such active imaginations,
        and think I should give a good raise
to my imaginary publicist.

I'm writing this with morning news on the radio
        and waiting for the coffee to be ready.
Mick, Scarlett, and Brad never showed up.

The sailors and bikers have all moved on.

Last message from earth

Dear spacefolk,
I saw you on TV as a boy in the 1960s.
You had insect heads, I remember,
and wore mylar suits.
Have styles changed much?
Peace to you, spacefolk.
We are beating up this planet
and there's always a battle going on.
All the humans, animals, plants and rocks,
even the water is turning bad.

It seems we're doing ourselves in.
I'm sorry if our ray-guns
and missiles hurt your spaceships.
We humans have big brains
but we don't use them very well.

Things are getting worse
since your last visit. I wonder,
does our planetary fear reach you?
Does our darkness radiate very far?
Are we known as that awful cancer
over in the Milky Way? Do you
have any idea what we should do?
We are now afraid of everything
and hope this doesn't infect your planet.
(Don't split more atoms than you need. *Big* mistake!)

Dear spacefolk,
I hope your people sing beautiful songs
and your children have hearts full of trust.
Please bring them by on your next visit,
earth will need their wonderful imaginations.

Humbled by the sun

"Everyone gets lighter, everyone is light." (John Giorno)

As heavy as the world is,
      there is always light.
You have to look for it.
With the current state of affairs
      this is absolutely necessary.

There is light you will find
      at the grocery store in the cereal aisle,
where a little boy has opened
a box of Cheerios
      and spread them all on the floor,
      his mandala of *oooooo*'s.

He invites you to join him
      in his joy to keep light,
to make lighter the weight of the world,
until we become light and lighter still
      in the brightness of day at noon,
still humbled by the sun.

The craft of poetry

"Life is lived only once. And the less seriously the better." (Paul Bowles)

Write about all you've squandered,
　　　　　of friends you've often loved
and strangers more often avoided.
　　　　　Take an eraser to days you'd rather forget.

Shine a light on your virtues,
　　　　　if you think you have any,
and write every day if boredom
　　　　　or the bottle doesn't stop you.

String words together on a page
　　　　　and see if they make remotest sense.
This is not an absolute requirement,
　　　　　but you'll spend more time

explaining the meaning of what you mean
　　　　　than on the meaning, if you follow me.
If you're able, prop up your weak chin
　　　　　with a beard to give your words authority.

That's it. Quite simple, really.
　　　　　Don't reach for prizes or acclaim,
and if you manage to earn a penny a word,
　　　　　occasionally you'll be able to afford

a cup of coffee at a restaurant.
　　　　　Abandon all hope of large-press publication.
You're better off passing bad checks
　　　　　if public notice is what you're after.

The starlings of Hollie Street

for Michelle

This winter the starlings
gathering in treetops
have been asking about you.
Are you eating well? Keeping warm?
Is your heart beating strong and sure
on your chosen flight?
The starlings of Hollie Street
Are making sure all's well with you.

The murderous-looking crows
still scatter the squirrels
who are looking for pecans
on the front lawn,
but their hearts don't beat the same
since you moved away.
Their perimeter march
lacks the cool precision
I imagine they once
performed for you.

There's a different music
in the bamboo; when the wind sighs,
it's lonely for your piano'd blues
out the kitchen door. Now,
when warm weather arrives,
you aren't there on the porch
with a tumbler of sweet Arkansas tea,
and the summer heat
finds me with a martini instead.

Nature adapts slowly, but all
of these signs are good.

The world in its poetry
will find the old truth in new songs
here on Hollie Street.
I tell the starlings
you're nesting on Pioneer Circle now,
and that you wish them well
from far-away Watkinsville.

They note another cat
has arrived to amuse them.
High in their perches
the starlings laugh easily,
out of reach of Cheesecake Louise
and her distance at the screen door.
All at once, as if on signal,
the birds rise up and scatter
with a great noise. I imagine
they are out in force, looking,
keeping high watch in the event
of your return. Hurry back soon.

Zoom

Whose dreams are these?
There are never any automobiles
or airplanes. I'm never writing.
These dreams belong to another time,
when nothing was written down,
a horrible fate for a writer.
I'm in someone else's idea

of a good time, but I'm never
a drunkard on Olympus delivering
divine messages. That's out
of my league. There's often music –
why Mozart? I'm not that old --
I'm spry and agile, I'm never older
in dreams,

but I'm always somewhere else
I can't quite place. Last Monday night
I was definitely someone else.
I dreamt about a class reunion
where everyone knew me
but I had no idea who they were.
Who are you?

Another night, and this one
was a bit scary, I swam across
the lake with my head under
water, I didn't have to breathe air.
In my waking life I can't swim,
so this wasn't me either.
Who am I?

What is the message of these dreams?

Why can't I be someone who inhabits
the Arts and Leisure section
of the Sunday *New York Times* -- a world of
premieres and reading all the new books,
a kind of cultural levitation?
That sort of flying would be fun.

I implore the dream editor
to lay off the senseless fantasies,
tell him give me *real* dreams
such as my mind can explicate,
and stop infesting my nights with
someone else's nonsense. I want to
be myself, only more so.

"No poems about cats"

*"The **cat** does not offer services. The **cat** offers itself." (William Burroughs)*

There, at the last, is the instruction
in the abrupt style of the young. Dismissive, a topic
beneath contempt of any serious poet:

"Absolutely no poems about cats."
What? You might as well command
thunder not to rattle your hat.

Mention your critical embargo
to Wallace Stevens and T.S. Eliot
and see where you go.

Even Burroughs, the old cat in the hat,
envied the con jobs of every sly tom
looking for shelter and a milk bottle:

"Someone said
that cats are the furthest animal
from the human model.

It depends on what breed
of humans you are referring to,"
he wrote, "and of course, what cats."

A writer must have words
about cats, his, or the world's.
Kerouac. Hemingway, of course. Twain:

"A cat is more intelligent
than people believe,
and can be taught any crime."

Who speaks for my old Dexter,
Dylan, or his sister Flame, whose rhyme
is worthy of a turn in any poem

as in a Broadway musical:
Grizabella's got nothing on the lady Flambeau.
And just so you know,

what of the unnamed, hysteric calico
who rattles nerves at three a.m.
with an aria outside your window?

Deny, deny you might,
but you'll get no sleep that night.
Papa Hemingway was right:

"One cat just leads to another."
Auden and his cat would tell you, too –
that is, if either of them cared enough to.

Beckett, and Ginsberg, William Carlos Williams,
Stephen King and Joyce Carol Oates,
PG Wodehouse and Robert Graves;

and here's Abraham Lincoln:
"No matter how much cats fight,
there always seem to be more kittens."

No poems about cats? Editor, then
perhaps it's best to state it plain:
he'd just as soon leave you out in the rain.

Consider Christopher Smart just for a start.
Turn down Ray Bradbury? Jean-Paul Sartre?
All right, editor, if that's not art

don't expect a reply from cat.
It doesn't matter if he's out or in.
No one really speaks for him:

"Dogs come when they're called.
Cats will get back to you on that."
That's the cat's *meow* there, Jim.

On time

Music is decorated time
       that hangs in the air

Computers suck up time
       as grass sucks up rainwater

Contemplating time usually
       means contemplating mortality

Time is a continuing story
       which mostly won't involve you

Even for the little while you are here
       time couldn't care less

Time used to go in circles
       with a face like a clock

Now time is simply a number
       with a series of dots

Spending time makes it sound
       like a man-made commodity

Yet somehow birds migrate
       by the passage of time

Whatever animals believe
       is true and correct

What time is it?

Mercury in retrograde

Listen: now is not so bad.
People had it just as tough
in so-called golden days.
There's no point in going back
to a simpler time. Things
were never so simple.
Back then, death was still
completely irreversible.

They charge for emotions now,
but back then when you had them
they cost as much, and impossible to trace
even when they were genuine.
They just descended, *whammo!*
Unpredictable as flashback.
Sadness or fear would twist
your face or crack your voice.
Tears would flow down your cheek.

Everyone was after the same things:
work, money, happiness, a good meal,
not necessarily in that order.
We wanted to save our faces.
Now you can just get a new one.
I can remember when the pursuit
of unhappiness was a privilege.

Heart condition

Given enough time and pressure
       the heart can turn into
the hardest rock, a weight
       made of overworked goo:
a keeper of faults
       and unlived-up-to promises,
       its beating a passing measure,
a ledger of who owes who,
who did what to whom, and why.

Fist-sized,
clenched,
until it opens.

The heart's true condition,
       for each and all to know
as daylight turns to night,
       is the forgiven slight
and kindness returned;
       to hear the tiniest sound
       of heart's ice breaking
with a force so unexpected
it cracks the hardest stone in two.

Blue o'clock

It was blue o'clock when I heard
      the dog barking, racing down the street
toward my house, racing to where
      he knows the cats live under the porch.

My porch. Here he comes, that black lab
      who wouldn't know an old shoe
from a softshoe, yelping for joy,
      hoping to surprise the cats at breakfast.

From twenty feet behind comes the woman
      dragging the leash behind her. She's wearing
flowered pajama bottoms and a tee-shirt
      that advertises Jack Daniel's on it,

walking as slowly as if her feet
      are working in muscle memory. She's
done this walk a hundred times, I bet.
      "C'mere, you, c'mere," she yawns.

I open the porch door and wave at her,
      neighborly. "Here," I say, and point to the lab,
who is stuffing Meow Mix in his jaws.
      "That must be some good cat food,"

the woman says. "He likes it a lot."
      "Mm-hmm," I agree, as she gets the leash
around Boo's neck at last, and struggles
      to drag him away down the street, barking.

The cats slowly reappear, one by one.
      I pour out more food, and then some cream
in a saucer. "Here," I yawn. "Morning, kids."
      And that's the 7 a.m. neighborhood news.

Alternative universe

If there is an alternative universe
I'd like to visit now. If it's right next door
I'll go and introduce myself
and ask for some sugar,
just to meet the neighbors with their two heads
and four hands
– imagine playing the piano! –
and find out
if life in this other world
has been any better for them,
if skies have been more blue.

Who knows? Just in case their universe
is filled with heartbreak as our own,
I'll sit on their porch and commiserate
about the nosy neighbors who make
things just as bad for them.
Then I'll offer a pull from the bottle
of whiskey I have in my back pocket,
which will burn in their throats at first,
but make their world a little less tough.

Tao Jones

These summer days I close my eyes
        at 4 p.m., make a martini, and a wish:
that all the money in the world disappears
        leaving humanity to discover empty wallets.
This would make the real cashless society
        with nothing to sell but all for barter,
the clothes off our backs for real necessities,
leaving our souls naked for neighbors to see.

How would society value itself without money,
        the slips with *In God We Trust* making avarice
a religious belief? America, take your hands
        off your wallet and look beyond Dow Jones
at 4 p.m. for your daily worth. Surprise your neighbor
with a free, naked dance in the front window!

A sonnet to the Board of Elections of Clarke County, Georgia

I hope this election season finds you well.
I mailed my ballot with choices marked
appropriately in black ink, circles precisely filled,
and proper first-class postage affixed, although
I consider this a poll tax upon my suffrage.
Well and done. I see by the Secretary of State's website
my ballot has been received and approved,
although it may not be counted until November.

It seems a little silly to wait so long to tabulate
a paper ballot safely delivered by the US Mail,
that 19th-century institution, as our once-sturdy democracy
seems to be in such dire straits here in the 21st.
Be that as it may, I remain confident my electoral privilege
has once more been successfully fulfilled. All best.

Ashes and diamonds

for Aralee Strange

Here's a timber dance to your word of mouth,
where poets drink whiskey straight from the jar.
All in attendance at your rough court
bear their trinkets and diadems,
fetch leather jackets and cigarettes,
hoping to be struck by the lightning flash
of your Alabama laugh.

Ventriloquists throw rhymes to rafters,
lovers cast hopeful spells, and madmen
break vows of silence they hold for years
like monks. Your punks and priestesses
make a felt, strange poetry,
mixing your ashes with their diamonds
in the heart's red wind-up toy.

For Aralee, then, a poet's incantation.
Here I pour tea from a porcelain cup
into vast seas of Chevrolets and clouds,
spin a radio dial for Hank's real lovesick blues,
consult a Ouija board for nouns and verbs.

I spread these words like seeds on water
where maybirds take them to your new Globe,
so the lands mapped by their roots and branches
will ring your Ohio River'd fingers.

The epistle of the deer in the bamboo

Last night I wandered, lost in the thicket
of bamboo over where the sun sets.
I had been lost for many hours.

I didn't know if it was the promise of food
or a stream of water I found there once.
I might have dreamed this, I was so tired.

I was alert to the air, to the presence of humans
I knew were there within their houses.
I made my way forward out of the thicket.

As I stood there, my breath calmly measured,
there was much I saw for the first time clearly.
There was a clear way before me,

as if a place I had been seeking.
Sure of myself as I had never been,
I moved forward knowing this is what I wanted.

Yet the strangest of things occurred:
the more I had all of this within my reach
the more the light suddenly shifted,

so that the surface of truth began to alter itself.
Was I deluded? No, I could see the truth ahead
as clear as blue sky. That remained unchanged.

The closer I approached the clear path
the less I understood was the truth
and the more I became fascinated

with shadows that dappled the way.
I could not understand the pure truth,
and the shape of its form beguiled me.

It hurt to think that this was the truth itself
made of a million broken pieces,
that I was a part of it in my own stumbling way.

I made my way back into the thicket.
There I felt safest, away from the clear path,
comforted in the bamboo's familiar form.

Then the bamboo, their bark, with dark roots behind,
flew upward each with their own shadow,
and left the blue sky standing.

New Father Time (to Allen Ginsberg)

Dear Allen

I wonder what you would do
 if you were here this new years eve
  I'm happy to report
   handsome boys still ride the crosstown bus
    read poetry and smile at strangers
    who smile back

angry words are still written down and spoken
 from stages and street-corners that speak truth to power
  and jazz still plays in basement doorways
   (Miles
    Monk
     Coltrane's giant steps)
      while streetlights bestow halos on panhandlers

and there's money in the bank
 but business says it's not enough
  and there's money in the halls of Congress
   but business says it's not enough
    and there's money in the media
     but business says it's still not enough

enough never seems to be enough
 in a country that always has too much
  this last december week
   in this cold december year

. . . . .

Dear Allen

I wonder what you would think
　　of what America's done with the 21st century
　　　　the country always wants more
　　　　　　but it already has too much
　　　　　　　　The country still gets what it
　　　　　　　　　　wants and still gets never enough of what it needs

America never gets enough hope
　　like America never gets enough of anything
　　　　bank industry auto industry housing industry
　　　　　　not enough of bailouts
　　　　　　　　business says $700 billion is still not enough of money
　　　　　　　　　　all America gets is more but it never gets enough

America never gets enough war
　　two world wars not enough of wars
　　　　war on terror not enough of war terror
　　　　　　war in Korea and Vietnam wars in Iraq and Afghanistan
　　　　　　　　not enough

America never seems to get enough
not enough of saints in Dallas and Memphis
　　not enough of saints in Montgomery and Selma
　　　　four little girls not enough saints in Birmingham church bombing
　　　　　　three dead not enough saints in 1964 Freedom Summer
　　　　　　　　while those guilty of murder walked free for decades

America only gets more
it never seems to get enough
　　not enough saints in Oklahoma City bombing
　　　　not enough saints in World Trade Center collapse
　　　　　　two thousand dead not enough saints from Katrina flooding
　　　　　　　　America never gets enough of its saints
　　　　　　　　　　in this home of the brave

America only gets more
it never seems to get enough
    countless dead lynched from trees or dragged behind trucks
        numberless beaten shot stabbed and gasoline bombed and burned
            gay teens dead from suicide who never know it gets better
more abortion clinics bombed and their doctors killed
    because legally women have the audacity to choose
        America never gets enough human rights
          in the American dream

America only gets more
it never seems to get enough
    more corrupt politics is not enough
        more chest-thumping red-white-and-blue is not enough
          more boots on the ground hoo-hah is not enough
            more WikiLeaks documents
              exposing global secrecy and deception
              is definitely not enough

America never seems to get enough
it only gets more
    more shouting in the media and more manipulation
        more anonymous comments left on websites telling people
          who remember history to STFU
            more anonymous political money from big corporations
              that now have the rights of citizens

America only gets more
the country never seems to get enough
    of buying power with money in the halls of Congress
        of bribing watchdog groups with lobbyist donations
          of politicians telling voters only what they want to hear
            and not what they need to know

America never seems to get enough
it only gets more
 of election-year politicians targeting opponents with gun-sights on maps
  and telling their partisans go ahead and take aim
   of media companies that misinform and distort
    the truth for ratings with unfounded fear
     of media deception for political gain
      and money in the bank
       while the real facts go unreported

America only gets more
 more media spin is never enough
  in this 24-hour news cycle

America never seems to get enough
it only gets more
 more Congress talk not enough of congressional talk
  more Reagan/Bush era sweet talk not enough of sweet talk
   more Bush/Cheney era false talk not enough of false talk
    Obama/Biden reach-acrosss-the-aisle compromise
     is definitely not enough of tough talk

America only gets more
it never seems to get enough
 enough of coffins arriving at midnight at Dover AFB
  enough of FBI secret files on Nobel peace-prize winners
   enough of CIA leaks revealing secret identities
    enough of State Department secret dealings
     with enemies and terrorists who hide
      in countries whose oil America wants

America only gets more
    but it never seems to get enough
        of too much poverty
            of too much homelessness
                of too much joblessness
                    of too much hopelessness
                        of too much inequality
                            of too much irresponsibility
                                of too much hypocrisy
                                    in the land of the free

all America ever gets is more
    but it never gets enough
        enough is never enough
            in this American millennium

. . . . .

Dear Allen

I'm proposing you new Father Time
    for this third millennium
        a thousand-year party
            no more blackrob'd old man icon
                no more ancient doddering fool
                    no more hourglass or crook'd scythe

in Prague 1965
    you were King of the May *Kral Majales*
        this should be a piece of cake
            what d'you say

you in your top hat stars & stripes
    with harmonium at your side
        bearded smiling (or serious too

in hornrimm'd glasses)
                with a young man always there
                        ready to hoist yr pump organ

the new millennial hip Father Time
        what d'you say
                satisfaction guaranteed
                        or your millennium back

· · · · ·

Dear Allen

I wonder what you're doing this new years eve
must be some crazy scene
Jesus & Mohammed
                Coltrane blowing "Ascension"
                        Walt putting the moves on Neal
                                Jack and Gutauma discussing the dharma
                                    you and Peter rolling the joints
                                        (finest gage at low low prices)

imagine the conversation
        poetics and transcendence
                a love supreme ... a love supreme ...
                        (pls tell Mr Whitman we share the same
                                birthday   May 31)
later it's no time for talk
        party hats askew after serious drink
                give Jack that bliss'd out sloppy kiss
                        let Bill cop the immaculate fix
                                keep Neal away from the hydrogen jukebox
                                    but let him drive the bus

most of all New Father Time
slip America the dope of hope
this new year's eve
    let there finally be enough
        let there be more than enough
            let there finally be hope enough

give America the big-hope midnight kiss
    to last a thousand years
        to last a thousand years
            to last a thousand years
                let there finally be hope enough
                to last a thousand years

Let there be enough America to get it right
    let there be enough courage to get it right
        let there be enough responsibility to get it right
            give us enough love to get it right
            and enough sight

give us enough compassion to get it right
        give us enough time to get it right
            give us enough daylight to get it right
        and enough night

Your papers, please

Show me your driver's license and registration . . .
I can only close that account with a death certificate . . .
I have no record you're registered to vote . . .
Your student ID is not valid identification.

Show me your green card . . .
do you have your certificate of divorce?
May I see your passport . . .
I'll need your medical records, test results.

Do you have your receipt, raincheck, tax returns,
birth certificate, court summons, report card,
the deed, your fishing license, current utility bill,
prescription, proof of income, insurance card,

proof of income, occupany permit, military ID,
the ruling, your term paper, your dissertation,
parking voucher, social secrity card,
hall pass, permission slip, nurse's excuse,

bus pass, library card, credit card, DNA results?
Keep your hands where I can see them.

Clock strike

The clocks in the house
all go on strike
and argue with each other
more than I like.

The two in the kitchen
never quite agree;
is it ten past the hour,
or quarter-past three?

Even the clock in the radio
disagrees a third time.
It's not quarter-past,
it's 3:09.

I wish all the clocks
would learn to agree,
join a time-keepers' union
for a small fee,

but I'm sure they'd bargain
for some extravagant pay.
You can't get good help
For cheap these days.

News item (from a great height, April 21, 2010)

Samuel Clemens: November 30, 1835-April 21, 1910

Your correspondent here reports
  that *Clemens* has laid aside his pen.
Having arrived on Mr. Halley's comet,
  the author has it by the tail again.

His surprise at this astounding feat
  can not be overstated in the least;
he was quite prepared to make the journey –
  but not so much *deceased*.

Mr. Clemens says he is unafraid of heights,
  and enjoys St. Peter's good cigars.
Until wires are arranged, he sends regrets
  telegrams will be fewer from these stars.

The author is off in search of a dark saloon.
  Until then, I remain, your reporter
and most far-flung correspondent,
  Twain.

Buddha says

Open your palm I want to give you a stone.

The stone may be wisdom
or it may not, it depends
on what you do with it

some stone waits to be sand
waits to be mirror
waits to be telescope glass
waits to be mud

what is below the mud?
dirt / dust / gravel
but stone waits to be stone again

try and spend a lifetime asking
the right question
instead of seeking the wrong answer

ask the stone
why it wants to be stone
and you will have your answer

Magic spell

"Each dance and its music belong to a time and place" (Gary Snyder)

This morning I was listening to Vivaldi
        when I heard an unfamiliar note
and I thought, well,
maybe I was imagining things.
        At six a.m. these things occur.
            But there it was again.
I didn't dream that beautiful note
        a second time, did I?

I turned down the Vivaldi – the Four Seasons,
        as it happens, the Spring.
And there, on the branch outside
the window, a mockingbird
        sat improvising on the score.
            But when I turned the music down,
he flew away. He had been listening
        to the music, its magic spell.

Time looks best on you

I once had a future more than a past;
each tomorrow meant more than the last.
What happened next is easy to say:
tomorrow was always as fun as today.
Tomorrow, tomorrow, the dreamer's dream,
promised as a cat's bowlful of cream.
What's left to do is left to do.
May time in its passing look best on you.

Days may fly and days may drag
and everything inward may outwardly sag.
Friends will come and friends will go,
until no one knows what you surely know.
Sing and laugh at what tomorrow may bring;
as long as you're able, let the bells ring.
With each passing day, do what you do;
may time in its passing look best on you.

Nightstand notebook

The sleepy ears of night
hear the ghosts of day
still rattling the rafters

every evening a little death
and transfiguration
while the radio hums Strauss

overcome with frustration
it's time to sing a few songs
or learn a new one

e pluribus unum --
how often do I have to fall
for that old line

maybe I'll wake up
and be back in America
again

August

Rain shakes the bamboo in the yard,
the news is bleak and politic.

The sky is low; clouds in the west
promise a soaking before night is through.

Books on the nightstand promise dry land,
an escape from the dim day's bad turn.

Dinner dishes in the sink soak
while I read ten pages by lightning bolt.

Then, too dark to read, the lowered night
rattles the screen door with more wind:

close door, latch bolt, count the hairs on my head,
listen to rain try to drown me in my bed.

Prom night of the paperbacks

A man re-arranges the free paperbacks
on the revolving racks at the Athens library. He
puts all the books by male authors in one rack,
and works by women writers he moves to the other.

The library staff watch as he does this
and never interfere or ask him why,
but I like to think the gentleman
has a strict idea of propriety and order.

This is a way of keeping the flood of print and paper
set to his rule against the chaos of the word.
The staff have never seen him check out a book
or read in comfortable chairs nearby.

Once his task is done, and the books
are separate by gender on each rack,
the chaperone slips quietly away
leaving the dancers to the dance.

What are the odds?

It could have happened.
It had to happen.
It happened earlier, later,
it happened but not to you.

You were saved because
you were the first, last,
alone, or with others.
You were there, or not.

There was no one there,
or it missed you by an inch.

Because it was raining,
or the sun was in your eyes.
A step, a turn, a quarter inch.
Healthy, or sick and missed it.

Because, although, despite.
What would have happened
an instant later, happened a mile away.
A hairsbreadth escape.

You were on the left. The right.
-- *What was I thinking!* --
you were in or out of luck.

Now and zen

"What am I doing to disturb the inner peace that I already have?" (D.T. Suzuki)

I want a new now
        this one seems broken
with too much news
        and not enough zen

too much cause
        with too much effect
and tomorrow crashes
        into today again

without a breath
        to think about how
without a doubt
        I'm here and I'm now

better to turn off
        the news 24/7
and think about Blake
        sitting in Heaven
and all of the poets
        who lived then and live now
and wrote down their visions
        for all to follow

bathe for an hour
        in the impermanent stream
drink at the well
        of the impractical dream
(don't ignore the present
        things are as they seem)
do what you must
        keep the universe clean

zen and again
        when the heart seems hollow
sweep a clear path
        yourself to follow

Confound and amuse

(for Chris)

Here's a twist: I took a woman to the Christmas party once.
    (I like to mix things up, this makes life interesting.
        It confounds your enemies and amuses your friends).

Two hours before the party, a mutual friend
    used his one phonecall from the county jug
        to bail him out of jail. What to do?

He was so holiday drrunk the cops found him with his bike,
    parked on a railroad trestle whistling the Stones' "Get Off My Cloud,"
        happy as a . . . well, a holiday drunk.

Mine was the only phone number he could remember.
    Ahh, I had to rescue him of course -- a point of honor.
        Cathy understood -- and we made it to the party

at the Atlanta Ritz-Carlton eventually:
        Cathy in her sparkling, floor-length blue dress,

and I in my blue Atlanta Raceway sweatshirt and jeans,
        a two-day growth of beard, smelling of Fulton County jail.
        Confound and amuse.

Why I have a cat

I have a cat so I can accuse her of anything
(and everything)
and she'll admit to hiding things
where she thinks
I'll never find them. I'll scour the house
looking for keys / glasses / smartphone
(I put *right there*
to remember where I put it)

I realize then
the endless process of hide-and-seek
Cheesecake wants me
to find the toy mouse she lost
in the bedroom
which she receives with quiet reserve
just as I see my / smartphone / is next to her
battery charging

Stop-time

My heart beating, my blood running,
the light burning, my mind turning;

the clock's quick-ticking
time is moving. Time is passing.

Time is perpetually perishing,
time is farewell each second;

time is eternal, time is lessened.
When we are in step, time is flowing,

controlling pace before we get old,
even as we walk the receding road.

Stop-time, and make it stay
in the middle of the blazing day;

wave it from your warm brow, say
stand still with me even as time refuses.

All is moving, time cannot stand still;
time is farewell, time is farewell.

Calculation

Some nights
I'm wide awake at 4 a.m.
while the cat around my knees
breathes in quiet sleep.

Maybe I should just get up
and put some coffee on,
get a grip on the new day
and wrestle it to the ground,
but I'm too wired already.

With this energy
I could fix a lot of things:
the dripping faucet in the bathroom,
maybe rewire that broken lamp,
solve the calculus of world peace
or pay some bills.

Instead I'm staring
at the ceiling fan thinking
about the useless things
and things I can't fix at all
the whereabouts
of past lovers who left after fights
or because I didn't say no.

My sister who
was too young to die of cancer.

The woman outside
the train station who
asked me for a smoke
for the fourth day in a row.

I could have been nicer,
she really needed the change,
but I was late and this
isn't a walking town.
As I hurried past her
she said very clearly to me
you are really ugly
I turned around
and said *Lady, I don't even know you.*

She began to cry
she said *I'm really sorry,*
but I need some change
when I gave her a dollar
she folded it neatly and put it
in the pocket of her jeans.

Today I'll see her again
and she'll ask me for the money.
Will she ask for the dollar
before I offer it?

It's four a.m. where x is always the unknown.
I'm lying in bed wide awake,
trying to solve the human equation
one sleepless night at a time.

Library book sale

Okay, I'll just take a quick look.

. . . As if I need more books! I haven't read
the ones I bought at the last sale! Look! *Fallingwater
in Plans and Photos.* I need to buy
another coffee table for more coffeetable books.

Here's two rows of cookbooks . . .

. . . but I haven't made a single dish of pho saté
from the Vietnamese cookbook I bought
two years ago! *Middle Eastern Cuisine I Love*
looks interesting though. I like yogurt.

. . . uh-oh, a whole wall of CDs!

. . . all for a dollar each. Oh, I . . . well . . .
I'd enjoy the Sibelius symphonies.
I'll just buy these five and stop there.
Let's see, I'd better check my wallet.

. . . ah, perfect! Here you go. Thanks!

Sir, would you like a larger bag for all that?

Non-political politics poem

If the world doesn't explode
      think of all that tossing in bed
            all the sleep that's been missed
                  and the dreams lost instead

There's no point in living
      with such useless dread
            if the idea of tomorrow
                  is all in your head

And if that day never comes
      it will always be said
            he looked so peaceful
                there in his bed

November dark

First the ears give out
        then belief is suspended
then the stock market plunges
        then the tablecloth begins to fray
and chairs fall apart.
Doors fall off their hinges
        the cats start speaking in tongues
and I say "one at a time,
        in English, please" but they don't
        seem to understand.

It's November dark at 6 p.m.
        the sky itself begins to look old
the trees wail and begin to rattle
        producing bags of play money
        the president says I can keep.

It won't do me any good
        when rain starts hissing like snakes
and rivers begin running backward
up the hills from where they came
        and I'm wondering how much time

I have before the universe collapses.
        I should have packed a suitcase
long before this and the buses
        have stopped running. By now
it's too late to warn people
of everything falling apart.
        I hope the smart ones know this
and are sounding the alarm
        but when I look on Facebook everyone is
        glamorous and having a good time.

Sidewalk dharma

Look where you are going, not where you have been,
      though that too is a lesson.
            Walk with deliberate intent where you are headed,
                  even if you are guessing.

But watch your step – the Buddha would tell you
      it's how you walk, not when you arrive.
            Are you afraid? Oh well, you'll see
                  it's better to trip and fall than just to survive.

Hurt and pain are the day's real test.
      If you fall down, get up again –
            don't heed the path, and life's a real mess.
                That's a lesson with a knee's little twist. And then

whoops, whoops, you're down again. So what?
      As Beckett says, fail better next time.
            We all get where we're going, simple as that,
                and no one said that life's a straight line

except to the grave. That's the lesson, sure
      as the days follow one another.
            The end is still the stumble without fail or cure.
                So go carefully, one foot in front of the other.

Snow sonnet

The sleeping dogs don't see the beauty of the snow
      as it falls at midnight, or its whiteness so stark.
            We stand in awe at the new-frosted window
                  watching the barn as it disappears in the dark.

The stillness that descends upon us
      mounts hourly in drifts
            deep as the year that ends upon us.
                  We go to bed. Overnight the world shifts

on an axis swung from pole to pole,
      from dark to light, as we go on dreaming.
            A southern snowfall uncovers the soul:
                  The garden rake, left out and leaning

on the shed, has a cardinal on it.
      His red is my heart with snow upon it.

Unlucky charm

Unlucky me, who has the time
to read all the books on my shelf;
this covid quarantine allows me
to think about what I am doing,
have done, and will likely do again.
Horrible. The once-fleeting thought
now takes up all my time;
the daily grind is now a chore
of things I have all done before.

It's beautiful springtime outside my door.
The cats roll lazily on the walk,
neighbors wave as they stroll by.
Locked down, I venture to the porch
– that far! – with magazine and glass,
wave at them as they pass, the least
of neighborliness I can manage.
I find ways to avoid the news, the virus,
the lack of any plan.

The strangeness of going nowhere
for a month or more makes sense;
my mind is nothing if not sensible,
avoiding a plague by staying home, defensible.
Yet I'm slowly learning the necessity
and simple pleasure of being *somewhere else*.
Until the danger passes, I'm my own enemy:
I have the unlucky charm of my own company.

Looking for the tigers

for Steve

Philadelphia in a windy March.

The hometown boy, now 60 in suede jacket and cap,
throws his aching shoulders toward the wind and walks
his old boxer walk down even older streets: Kater to 20th,
then South Street past familiar accents, sidewalks of broken brick,
the windows advertising halal chicken and watch repair.

He points out the landmarks he knows too well.
That way is McGillins, if we should stop in for a pint.
Down Arch Street is Chinatown and the cherry blossoms.
Now he sees them every day disappearing in glaucoma.
We're on our way to the natural history museum

with its dinosaurs and butterflies, where a desert tiger behind a rock
is ready to pounce on deer who are suddenly alert.
The museum is a world grown large enough to see
everything big, close up, behind glass or suspended above us

inside man-made spaces. It's a world in control
unlike the wild lights and city streets outside,
the corner carts selling cheese steaks and gyros.
There are open cellar grates that lie in wait for uncertain footing
and a misplaced step. Watch for bicycles.

We're old college friends from 40 or more years ago.
Me with cerebral palsy watching my step, too,
at every turn in an unfamiliar city in winter wind.
At busy intersections I feel his hand on my back.
On cold marble steps he asks if I'm ready to try.

I test my balance slowly, one step at a time
touching the pale wall on my left carefully
while we walk down talking about our younger selves.
He reminds me I once made a pass at him in college.
I laugh at the memory and still remember the snow,
his flannel jacket, and how warm I imagined he'd be
to lay next to in another winter season.
Now we're just two old friends both on vacation
stumbling through a museum each in our peculiar gait.

We fumble over menus in restaurants, look for misplaced glasses,
and talk about life like old partners reunited,
as if we're finally seeing the entire world behind glass,
now big enough to see at last like a museum display.
Back at home he sinks into an easy chair. He's tired,

and the boxer's body that was once his own
now belongs to shots and aches and doctor bills.
I wear slippers to keep off the March chill.
We both walk slower these days but with more purpose,
two friends talking about poets and reading and art.

But we're always looking for the tigers who will pounce on us both
like unsuspecting prey alert behind museum glass. They're waiting.
We each tell ourselves we're ready for them all, the beasts
we know we'll never see coming around the corner of day.

Magic machine

I wish Zuckerberg
        had told the senators
                "my magic machine
                        is much like a mirror.
The more you gaze at it
        your self will appear;
                all for a small
                        and bloodless fee –
it's an American machine,
        as this august group
                will doubtless agree."

Instead all the senators
        believed the nicely-dressed boy
                when he said he was sorry
                        and it wouldn't happen again.
Something surely had to be done,
        but he didn't know what
                and he didn't know when;
                        and he left the room
without telling them how
        his darn machine worked,
                exactly, then.

Periodic table of poetry

"on poets who recite in public – and other sinners" *(Juvenal)*

Homer, of course and Aristophanes
        drunk Anacreon in Heaven
        Sappho in bits and pieces
what's left
tragic old Sophocles
        who wrecks Oedipus
        Virgil composes
while Ovid metamor-
        phoses

Willie the shake
        lost Milton then regained
Dickinson and Whitman swinging with
        Frost in his birches
Eliot with his trousers rolled
        Ez at the window of St. Elizabeth's, old
        Auden with his cigarette and bedroom slippers
        padding down Fifth Avenue, cold
Lowell and Berryman drunk at the bar
        Philip Whalen and his Chinese verse
Kerouac passed out in the car
        Ginsberg and Bukowski way out here
Diane di Prima no problem
        Adrienne Rich diving into the wreck
        Audre Lorde who said it was simple

Snyder in his Kitkitdizze
        who will outlive us all

then you
and me next

         ". . . it's someone else's turn to speak" – *Ginsberg*

One hundred

for Annette

I celebrated a friend's one-hundredth birthday
      with family who had traveled miles
and local folk just up the country road.
      The tea was sweet, the talk was sweeter,
while we took turns chatting
      and the honored guest
      sat quietly in the shade

Her mind is elsewhere now, occupied with years.
      We are repeated names with faces she can't place,
and she asks each in turn
      if we know how old she is.
"I'm one hundred!"
      she answers herself gleefully.

Husband, daughter, sons, their children, friends
      assemble for cake. Her eyes brighten
when she sees me. "Do you want to get married?"
      she asks, and grabs my hand. Then:
". . . my daughter is sixty-five. You look young.
      How old are you?"
      I laugh and tell her I'm sixty-three.
"Too young!" she says quickly,
      and turns away to blow out the candles
      that spell 1-0-0.

January flu

Hiding from the world with January flu
    is the best thing for a week or two.
Holidays are over and bills come due,
    you're in bed with nose-wipes and medicine too.

A cup of tea with some whiskey in it
    will set you straight – if just for a minute.
Then it's off to dreamland where there's no limit
    to what your clogged noggin has in it.

What scares you most is sure to be there
    nesting in cranium and roots of your hair,
or hiding in wait beneath some surrealist stair
    to give you the sweats in chilly night air.

Sooner or later you'll have to surface
    to make tea, or some other purpose.
You can't hide forever, no matter how worthless
    the month of January and its snottiest curses.

Once you've beaten the first-month flu
    you'll remember how many things you must do.
Start with some lines for a poem or two
    and hope February won't have its own wretched due.

Deal with the devil

Forget the other six of them, says Pride,
they're just using you.

Lust is a real looker, that's true,
but you can do better.

Avarice fills his cheap wine
when he thinks no one's looking.

The food in this place is so bad
even Gluttony can't finish his meal.

Sloth can't be bothered to push away
from the table for his nap.

Envy just eyes your plate hungrily,
and Anger is already arguing over the bill.

Be gone, all of you!
I'm the only one here who leaves a decent tip.

High summer still life

I'm up before the sun rises above the trees,
to open doors catching night in quiet surprise.

The cat is asleep in a wicker chair.
These are mornings without idea, first,

in simple starlight and a low moon,
not even bird sound to strike the note.
The night is passing without regret or prayer.

Before the day begins in earnest, let
the night recede in dreams and cool air.

Today I'll make plans that go wrong, measure
relationships that do not fit, find a shoelace broken.

These human faults I own. Right now,
these have nothing to do with the still life of morning.

Sit without light and watch the sky come down,
let it come down to fill the mouth and mind.
There is still time enough for light to build

above the roofline and the summer'd trees.
The sun will make the day without mistake.

If perfect

If perfect, love would be a crushing bore,
    and send us rushing to the door;
        stories of undying *amour*
            make insanity seem less of a chore.

Mankind is made for imperfection.
    How else explain love's indirection,
        and find in the heart's dissection
            the joys of every little indiscretion?

If by chance you win the human race,
    congratulations! Now the rest of us have space.
        Rejoice in the search, enjoy the chase,
            and look for love in every face.

Morning routines

The doe comes looking for breakfast.
      She's alone, old enough now
to be foraging on her own. I saw her,
      younger, her mother standing guard,
as she nuzzled in the fallen leaves:
      now the cats' food and water in the dish
are an invitation to them both,
      each keeping respect for one another.

The doe looks at me in the doorway.
      She steps back but doesn't spring away.
The cats, used to my morning watch,
      know there soon will be milk for them.
I'm such an easy touch. The deer, suddenly alert
      to a sound, still learning my daily routine,
bounds into the bamboo. She'll be back.

It rained in my sleep last night

and when I woke up this morning
the clouds were dark and wet

I thought the world was perfect-
ly in tune with my dreams

I knew for that one moment
how the gods must feel

Lit Kick replies

(The following efforts are replies to various poems posted in Levi Asher's website, Literary Kicks (www.litkicks.com), in the free-for-all creativity of the Action Poetry section. These were generally created in spur-of-the-moment reaction to the work of others, who are cited after each entry; craft was only a secondary consideration, taking a back seat to the Beat maxim of "first thought, best thought.")

Huis clos

"Hell
is other people,"
his echo replied.

(to bill_ectric: "Club web," 5/1/09)

Two rainbows over tea

Two rainbows over tea
get beat by a three-cloud straight
every time

(to jaimef, "news bulletin," 7/22/09)

Kentucky ham

After naked lunch
Bill & Joan had a little
Kentucky ham

(to dlt: "read Burroughs," 6/28/2008. Kentucky Ham is the 1973 novel by William Burroughs, Jr., 1947-1981).

Here in Ila, Georgia

Eleven-A is
just a blink
from Athens

home of R.E.M.and the
ancient greeks
(thanx Mr Byrne)

the crickets
dont chirp here
they murmur

(to dlt: "Cool," 8/22/09)

The five senses

are a temple of high regard.
While I pick tomatoes
in the garden

I'm sure to notice the butterfly
on the zinnia
with its stained-glass wings

makes
a most beautiful cathedral
too.

(to mickeyz, "in the name of the popcorn," 8/18/09)

Necessary things

the art
of composition

requires
a sharp pencil

and an even
sharper

memory

(to jaimef, "The Process," 2/10/10)

The old man

always has a few
astonishing tricks
up his sleeve

one is to be a young man
when the need
calls for it

(to mickeyz, "I was too amused to be afraid," 2/27/10)

Love

is a noun is a verb
is a tightness in the chest
that won't let go
even as you try
to release its grip
with your tongue

(to Snowqueen, "coversation," 6/7/2010)

Sometimes

the most courageous thing
people do
is just to walk down the street

sometimes the most
outrageous thing
is to let go of the desire for control

it might get you killed
but it can also
get you kissed

(to michaelamichael, "a snippet of my life," August 8 2010)

Carlo & Dean in Blake-time

"Mr Marx," said Mr Moriarty,
"what d'you think of Blake?"

"Well, I like his
experiences

better'n his innocences
but I'd sure take his

acid anytime"

(to ben209, "Mr. Carlo Marx." In Jack Kerouac's novel The
Subterraneans, *the name Carlo Marx was a pseudonym for Allen Ginsberg.
In* On the Road, *Dean Moriarty was a pseudonym for Neal Cassady.)*

At the grocery store pharmacy

I confront my sins at the machine
        that measures them all: my weight,
blood pressure, even body-mass index
        and whether I drink enough water.

The numbers aren't too bad:
        A little high here, a little low there,
but all in all a good mechanical report
        for a three-hundred nap checkup –

I never miss an afternoon nap.
        And my jeans still fit! Confidence!
Now I can schedule my annual physical
        and confess to my doctor.

Superhero in love

These days whoever opens my heart
    is wearing a mask, wielding lasers.

Listen, I once followed love
    across two whole continents
        in one afternoon.
That love turned out
    all wrong for me. That's right,
        that's how we did things back then.

But it was beautiful, that wrong love.
    You have to believe in innocence
        and the thrill of the chase.

Nowadays there can be a dozen of me
    at a superhero convention,
        so how will you know the right one?

Trust me, in you I can almost see --
    ah! Let me take your mask off first.

Sheltered in place

(Hurricane Irma, September 2017)

In a rising storm
>   I listen to the radio reports,
an old-fashioned way
>   of staying informed, while
reading Waley's *Translations*
>   *from the Chinese* --
ever-older information,
>   and just as current.

Weather
>   has been a source of wonder
and comfort for poets
>   across cultures: Li Po's mountain
and Snyder's Sourdough lookout
>   share the same awed view
of cloud and earth.

>   What view
I see from my couch
>   overtop of Waley's book
is the spray of rain
>   in bamboo, pecan trees
swayed and branches snapped
>   by wind at the window.
I'm sheltered in the moment
>   from the wild world.

"Kindle, registered trademark"

"In the time it takes to skim the bestseller list
you can wirelessly download an entire book."

That's an ad for the Kindle and the Kindle 3G, registered
trademark,
   on page 20 of the NYT Sunday Book Review of Feb 20, 2011.

The tagline for the Kindle describes my own self
   ten years previous: "Smaller! Lighter! Faster!"

but the ad makes me pause. I re-assess my own reading brain
   in its process: "Heavier ... leakier ... slower."

I appear to be letting more things in, the older I become,
   in the hopes that more ideas will stay put.

I read entire books, page by page,
   turning the pages slower than I used to. My brain

uploads in the curious reactions of synapse and nerve.
   I enjoy the texture of the printed page between my fingers,

the ink that still rubs off newsprint at the library
   and leaves fingerprint smudges on the cover of my Mac:

the inky identifier that marks me as a print reader, still.

I begin to notice more and more books in the library
   with their broken spines and torn covers, the plastic ripped,

as if they were buildings in the process of falling apart
   and ideas being let loose from windows of unbound pages.

No threat of the Kindle doing that. Its screen will only be blank
        when it fails: you won't be able to read a single downloaded word,

the ones and zeroes will be as indecipherable as dead language.

My mind processes entire books, page by page. It's taking longer,
        slower, and occasionally I trace a word with my finger, in awe

of a meaning I am not certain of. I am reading, not simply accessing,
        not scanning, not storing information to be tabulated and graphed.

Let the web be the great guardian of books: the exact phrase
        and the precise paragraph, the comma and the quotation-mark.

The Kindle, of registered trademark and sleek design,
        will give you the Dialogues of Plato, Reagan's speeches,

quantify the Adventures of Superman and Martin Luther King, Jr.,
        encyclopedize both Hoagy and Stokely Carmichael,

download Einstein in an instant. Facts are dead as tombs;
        an idea is still not responsible for what happens to it.

I read with all the faults that flesh is heir to.
        The Kindle can remember a million books

with its infinite ones-and-zeroes, but has it ever actually read one?

Back in the old neighborhood

Walking in the old neighborhood
    I see shadows of myself
        carrying groceries, waiting for a bus.

Now that I've moved away
    others have taken my place
        with the business of living

on a street I no longer think much about.
    An interviewer once asked
        the writer Paul Bowles, then 70

and living in Tangier,
    if he had memories of visiting
        his grandparents' house

in Elmira New York when he was six.
    Bowles surprised his questioner
        by describing each room in detail.

Amazed, the interviewer asked
    how often Bowles had been back
        to the house on Church Street.

"Oh, often," the writer replied instantly
    "I visit it in my dreams."

"I approve this message"

Friends, I urge you to run for public office.

Be a representative of yourself.
And when you cast a ballot for this high office,
vote for the candidate with your experience,

the one who understands you,
the candidate who is uniquely qualified
to represent you.

Your opponents with their hidden agendas
are in the race with truckloads of cash,
lobbyists, and ads,

ready to distort your record,
find fault with your principles,
make you unsure of yourself.

They have no plans for you.
Look them over, memorize their faces,
and then run like hell

to represent yourself.
A vote for you
is the only vote you can trust.

In the past
you may have elected yourself
and have been disappointed

in your own legislative record.
Forget that. Every election season
brings new challenges and fresh opportunity.

Voters have forgetful memories.
It's good to remember this simple rule,
and never record your illicit acts

of bribery, drug transactions,
or personal relationships.
These will wind up endlessly

on cable news, entertaining your enemies
and possibly ruining your career
unless your friends have deep reserves of cash.

When you enter the voting booth
choose the candidate with the most experience
in knowing where you stand on the issues.

Elect yourself. I approve this message,
and i serve as President of myself
as much as I can stand.

Coviderata (with apologies to Max Ehrmann)

Go masked amid the noise and haste,
       and strive to keep your nose covered.
As far as possible when you're in Trader Joe's,
       keep six feet distance from all persons.

Post your truth on Facebook without anger or using all caps,
       and scroll by others that are vexations to the spirit.
The world is full of deniers, so stay at home; there is happiness
       in binge-watching Hulu at 3 a.m.

You are a part of the Universe no less than Amazon or Netflix.
Use them.
       You have a perfect right to gain weight in quarantine.
And whether or not Covid-19 disappears like a miracle,
       the Universe is unfolding as it should even though you're
not in it.

Avoid sneezing. Use hand sanitizer.
       Gaze out the window with longing at the new normal.

Corner poets

"People are never ready to answer the telephone. Use poetry." (Jack Kerouac)

You won't find them in the Norton Anthology,
though they might be there under *Anon.*,

with words cribbed from Shakespeare, Yeats, Whitman,
four lines with more than a nod to Dickinson.

Corner poets work themes of life and death and love
into another millennium of ecstasy and heartbreak

but they won't be printed in the next edition.
Poet laureates won't know their names in conversation,

their work doesn't get read on NPR. The corner poets
are everywhere but in books.

Every city has poetry underfoot; at the bus stop,
posted on the coffeeshop wall. The poems

fly off loose-leaf pages at readings
for anyone to find, and offer no charge

other than to listen. Their words were once Sufi poetry,
chanted in defiance in Tahrir Square.

At days end the words are a wish calling us to bed,
offering nothing less than the moon in their arms.

Autumn cats

Autumn cats
play in bare trees
testing vantage points

One by one they climb
their conning towers
watching for birds

and nibble on dead leaves
leaving the branches
picked clean as fishbones

Wholeheartedly, Ort

(1950-2023)

There's an empty stool, at the Manhattan Bar,
where William Orten Carlton would hold court.

Generations of UGA students became his acolytes
learning more than any classroom could teach

about the delights of newly arrived beers,
all the post offices of Georgia,

and nearly forgotten names of the blues:
Hopeless Homer, and Hop Wilson and His Chickens.

Ort is off with another adventure in Van Ella,
uncharted now. I'm sure he'll arrive in time

for the next broadcast of Ort's Radio Problem.
Athens has plans to name its main post office

for William Orten Carlton, a fair tribute,
but I imagine an addition to the city seal:

his familiar closing, *Wholeheartedly*,
emblazoned at the top.

Sad to say, Athens will never again
exclaim "Hi, Ort!" except in our dreams.

Today tonight tomorrow

The end of the world is beautiful today.
Have we erased ourselves from the lives
that used to surround us in photos?
Will we begin over again,
seeing each other every day of the week?

....

Tonight reality is explained by the rain falling
while the Mets-Braves game murmurs
its eternal ritual on the radio, the benediction
of a come-from-behind win
as darkness settles on a late-game rally.

....

I was supposed to write, but didn't.
Tomorrow always promises I'll be ready
but creativity is usually not that charitable.
I'll try and wake with a dream to tell you,
but often find the page is blank.

"The modern Ulysses" (after Tennyson)

... It may be that the pints will wash us down:
      It may be we shall shop the discount aisles,
      And see the great Jamesons that we knew.
Tho' much is drunken, much is spilled, and tho'
We are not now the drinkers which in old days
      Drank the river down, that which we are, we are;
      One equal elbow on heroic bars,
Made weak by beer and bladder but strong in will
To call, to quaff, to pay, and not to yield.

Prodigal

On a final visit home I felt lucky,
and returned to my grandparents' house.

I was standing on the sidewalk long enough
to attract attention, I suppose.

A stylish young woman opened the door.
I told her I remembered the house

from the '50s, after my parents moved in.
"Oh, I see," she said quietly. Then:

"Tell me what you remember of it."
A test, just to be sure. I asked

if the entryway still had a red tile floor,
was the pass-through delivery box

still in the kitchen for milk deliveries,
a coal chute and box in the basement.

Was there a cedar closet in the upstairs hall?
Her face softened. That satisfied her,

and she asked if I wanted to look around.
I thought this over a long moment, deciding

that memory is one's luck for a lifetime.
"Oh, I see," she said again, more softly.

"You might want to check the closet
in the boys' bedroom though," I told her.

"There might be a letter from a ten-year-old
stuffed in a crack, second shelf up.

That will be my letter to the future.
You may get a kick out of it."

She smiled, considerate to a stranger on her doorstep.
"Yes, I'll be sure to read it," she said.

The space between

reality and illusion
our lives and our dreams
can be an ocean of salt

impossible to swim
without swallowing some truth

the balm of existence
depends on believing
that if you keep swallowing

the truth will turn
to honey in your mouth

A note of thanks

"Between thought and expression lies a lifetime" (Lou Reed)

For a writer of poems, the end is always just a beginning. If he's lucky the poem he's just written clicks together and the meaning tumbles out line by line, but there can always be the question of ideas left unsaid: "What did I mean here, exactly?" leads to many a sleepless night.

I have had many friends, poets, and total strangers help clarify the meaning of my poems. Public readings are often a terrific sounding board, and in that regard I thank the audiences of Athens, Georgia for their help. Globe Athens provides a wonderful place to try out new ideas every month, and never runs out of Guinness.

Personal friends can be relied upon to give a poet the best reports. They suffer through bad English, misplaced modifiers, and general confusion over where poems mean to go. Thank you Bob Ambrose, David Oates, Penny Noah, and Gene Bianchi for listening while I sorted out what I mean to say.

Family and friends offered terrific support and encouragement after the publication of my first collection, *Straw Hat Stanzas* (2022), also available through Parson's Porch Books. A portion of sales helps a food bank in Chattanooga TN and this current collection will help Parson's Porch Books continue in those important and necessary efforts. Thank you, David Tullock.

As Lou Reed put it in a simple phrase, creativity takes a lifetime of finding the right path between thought and expression. Every poet hopes to convey life and ideas in his work, and have it read. As readers, thank you for supporting the arts and those who find it a necessary part of life. Finally, with gratitude for his generosity and continued understanding, thank you, Dac Crossley.

Mark Bromberg
Athens, Georgia
June 8, 2024

about **Straw Hat Stanzas**
(Parson's Porch Books, 2022)

"Mark Bromberg's *Straw Hat Stanzas* (2022) is a delight, filled with truth and lives set mostly in Athens, GA. The poems come in many voices but with the kind of wisdom that only grows after a life filled with significant words and ideas. The reader senses real people behind the good times and difficult ones that Bromberg writes about. This is a fine achievement from a writer who knows what is important in the world." (Philip Lee Williams, author of *The Flower Seeker: An Epic Poem of William Bartram*)

www.ingramcontent.com/pod-product-compliance
Lightning Source LLC
Chambersburg PA
CBHW071019120626
46546CB00003B/1159